ISBN 978-0-332-77310-0
PIBN 11248716

... settle down.

Lines and more lines . . .

Court of laughs . . .

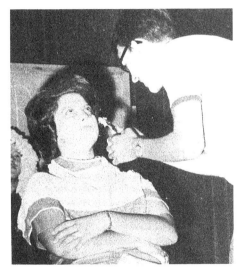

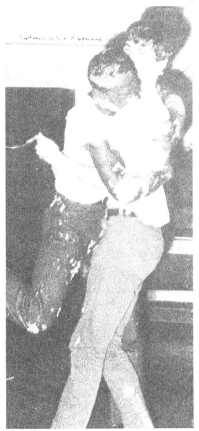

Society happenings . . .

. . . and a good time was had by all.

'The Unknown' rock out for Philo's Fall Dance.

Cook-out follows Clio hayride.

Speakers from near and far · · ·

Assemblies this fall featured Pres. Rackham and
ABC-TV's news commentator Peter Jennings.

Four-legged basketball . . .

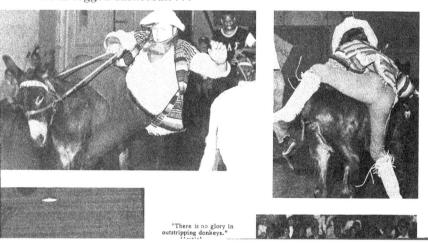

"There is no glory in
outstripping donkeys."

Bill Smoltz and John McCormack starred in Edward Albee's ZOO STORY.

C.P.B. sponsors Halloween dance . . .

"Dancing is wonderful training for
girls, it's the first way you learn to
guess what a man is going to do before he does it."
   Christopher Morley
   (1890-   )

Philo-Ferx weekend, 1968, promised
to be a highpoint of the semester. Heavy
rain, a fact of life here at McK, resulted
in the cancellation of the annual football
tilt and the post-game picnic. The pre-
game dance was held in Deneen Center
however and was enjoyed by all present.

Relaxation . . .

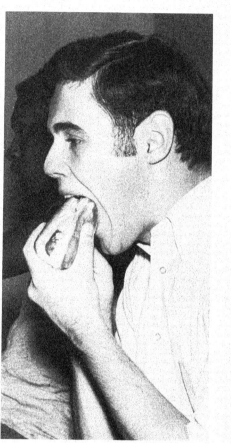

Jackson wins pool tourney . . .

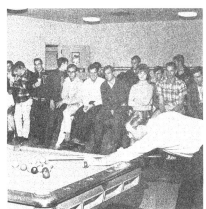

"Whoso neglects learning in
his youth, loses the past and is
dead for the future."
Euripides

Campus life features diversification . . .

(Above) The Howard Hanger Trio Performs jazz in Deneen Center.
A large audience was present for a program by Richard Shickel, noted
film critic. (Below).

The Student Congress Variety Show was an overwhelming success. The show, a benefit for the Holman Library, featured many varied acts, from rock to opera. The initiative displayed by the students demonstrates the interest they have in the future of McKendree College.

Homecoming '68

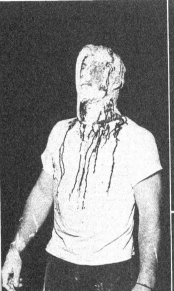

Jerry Zimmerman
Homecoming 1968's
"Ugliest Man on Campus"

21

Cafe nite features relaxed atmosphere

Dennis Burke receives the Vesely Scholarship Award.

Left: Bear Brand in action. Right: Al Fisher receives prize for 2nd Place. Below: The Queen candidates & the reigning Queen, and the 1968 Queen's court.

Coronation ceremonies . . .

Her Majesty, Miss Vicki Coleman, 1968 Homecoming Queen.

November 23, 1968, Miss Vicki Coleman was
ed as the McKendree Homecoming Queen.
Coleman is from Percy, Ill. and was escorted
e evening by Mr. Phil Schwab. The Queen's
and escorts are as follows: Far left: Freshman
Linda Everett and escort Bruce Roper. Far
left: Senior Queen Candidate Patti Knop and
Glenn Oliphant. Lower left: Sophomore Maid
Rutledge and escort Greg Snyder. Below: Ju-
Maid Maureen Rawley and escort Terry Florek.
right: Senior Queen Candidate Betsy Doer-
and escort Peter Saineghi. Right: 1967 Home-
g Queen Simone Daesch and escort Dave
n.

McKendreans dine and dance . . .

Other Homecoming activities . . .

Students caught in the act . . .

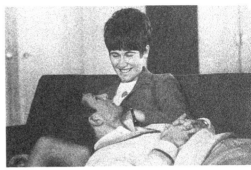

The **DMZ** adds a new dimension to campus life

Plato presents Walter Scott . . .

Plato was credited with a first when it presented, exclusive of the Campus Program Board, a concert with Walter Scott and the Kommotions.

and the beat goes on . . .

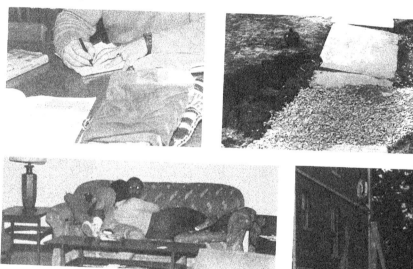

The president hosts faculty and students

Christmas at McKendree

Stu-Co sponsors party for underprivileged

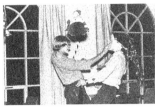

Snow . . .

Junior class auction for fun and profit

Right: Col. Chas. Alcorn auctions off "goodies" for the Junior Class. Below: Derek Hill receives his culinary prize.

Finals bring varied reactions

VANILLA FUDGE

Gabriel appears at McK . . .

Alexander Gabriel of the U.N. press corps speaks at Mc-
Kendree. Mr. Gabriel is known for his knowledge of foreign
affairs and policy.

Bearcats on NAIA trail to K.C.

McKendree begins 141st year

Lt. Governor Paul Simon, member of McKendree's Board of Trustees, gave the Founder's Day address. Lt. Gov. Simon spoke on the role of the small, liberal arts college in Illinois. Founder's Day 1969 was well attended by students, faculty, administrators and friends of the college.

Rest and relaxation

"Odd Couple" is a smash at McK!

Jack Farrow and Bill Smoltz starred in Neil Simon's "The Odd Couple."

The other side of McKendree . . .

Springtime at McKendree

50

Actor Conreid appears at McK

Hans Conreid, one of the most distinguished and versatile actors on the American theatrical scene spoke at McKendree during Fine Arts month. His presentation included readings from the Bible, Shakespeare, Wolfe, Lincoln and Heine.

April—Fine Arts Month

Left: Scenes from A WILDE EVENING WITH SHAW featuring Mayo Loiseau and Richard Gray. The program was comprised of the plays, essays and speeches of Oscar Wilde and Bernard Shaw. Below: Ron Bottcher, a leading baritone of the Metropolitan Opera, was also a featured performer during April. Right: Twenty-two year old Michael Lorimer, a classical guitarist, captivates a McKendree audience. Lorimer, a student of Andres Segovia, displayed his musical skill with a program of music spanning four centuries.

Mayo Lissow
essays and
ther, a leading
emer during
ical guitarist,
less Segovia,
four centuries.

Spring Formal 1969—"The Luau"

The expressions of John Streb and Judy Herrin are indicative of all who attended "The Luau" sponsored by the Juniors.

Student Congress campaign trail

Above: Presidential candidate Jay Hodges stresses a point during the Forum. Above right: A large crowd turned out for the "meet-your-candidates" Forum sponsored by Student Congress. Right: Pres. Elect Bob Greene shakes hands with Pres. Jerry Boner while Vice Pres. Elect Phil Schwab and Reps.-at-Large Smoltz, Herrin, Howie and Moore look on. Below: Junior class Reps. Westlund and Hogan and Senior John Streb discuss plans for the coming year.

McKendree hosts parents

McKendree College Parents Weekend 1969 was very well attended this spring. The parents were treated to shows of McKendree student abilities as well as to a concert by the "Time Square Two."

"The Arcade", run b
many hours of enter

"The Arcade", run by two McKendree students, provided many hours of entertainment.

"I say, my secretary must have left the window open again and allowed this feathered friend in."

PHI LAMBDA SIGMA WINS...

Above: The marathon runners about to "keck" off Greek Week 1969. Below left: Philo's Derek Hill poses before running his "leg" of the marathon. Below right: Ferox's Dave Rose hands off to Dean Schmalenberger who ran the final "leg" of the relay.

Friday evening independents as well as "Greeks" were treated to a "grecian banquet" and a skit show. Above right: Clio's fantastic half-dozen charge up the aisle. Below: Scenes from "the party" at the Ferox Laugh-In.

Philo men Owens, Keene and McKenzie bathe some poor soul in the waters of Horner Park.

Ferox's Dave Hampleman takes a breather after the sprints. Below: Adelphi's Dennis Swick wins the hundred yard dash.

Greek God, Steve Keene and Goddess, Cindy Upchurch were crowned at the dance Saturday evening. Below: Ferox's Jay Hodges as Dean Schmalenberger.

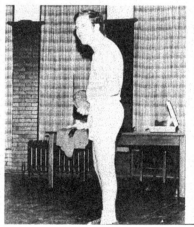

...GREEK WEEK 1969

Above: Adelphi's Chip Murray "splashes down" during the Mud Jump competition.
Below: A broken rope meant sprawling bodies Saturday morning at the Ferox-Philo tug-of-war.

Dr. Rackham becomes McKendree's 28th President

Commencement 1969

Above: Educator Lindley Joseph Stiles, the Inaugural speaker. Below: The class of 1969 advances and is recognized. Right: Dr. Robert I. White, the commencement speaker, President of Kent State University, Kent, Ohio.

Dr. Lindley Stiles and Dr. Robert White both received Honorary Doctor of Laws degrees. (above) Dr. Unruh is shown placing the hood on Dr. Stiles. (left) Mr. Akers placed the hood on Dr. White, shown here receiving his degree from President Rackham. (right) Below left: Dr. Rice places the hood on Dr. David Trueblood, the Baccalaureate speaker. Dr. Trueblood received the honorary degree of Doctor of Letters. Below right: Miss Barb North receives her degree from Dr. Rackham.

KNEELING: (left to right) Wayne Loehring, Max Hook, Terry Florek, Steve McFall, Dean Jackson. STANDING: Dave Williams, Steve Laur, Paul Funkhouser, Mike Finley, Dennis Korte, Steve Keene, Ed Belva.

68-69 Bearcats

Head Coach Harry Statham

Steve Keene

Wayne Loehring

Terry Florek

Max Hook

Dean Jackson

Dennis Korte

Steve Laur

NAIA Tournament 1969

McKendree College, long overlooked as a candidate for the NAIA District 20 tournament, upset tradition this year by bagging the No. 2 berth in this post-season event. The Bearcats' inclusion in the tournament marks its first invitation since becoming an independent team in 1963.

The first game of the tournament saw Chicago State fall to McKendree, a game played in Lebanon. A spirited team then traveled to Millikan University for the deciding game of who was to represent District 20 in the Kansas City finals.

Losing the game at Millikan was not an easy one, but everyone at McKendree is proud of their Bearcats and Coach for having such a fine season. Next year--it will be "all the way to K.C."

Mgr. Bob Drews, left; Head Coach Dave Dutler, right.

69' Bearcats Baseball Team

KNEELING: (left to right) Robert Drews, Mgr., John Mule, Nick Passomato, Dennis Korte, Jerry Boner, Bill Foster, Tony Musso. STANDING: Dave Dutler, Coach, Howard Thomas, Mike Fenton, George Fuiten, Terry Florek, Jim Nail, Dennis Swick, Terry Etling, David Musso.

**P
I
T
C
H
E
R
S**

Left to right; Nick Tropiano, Tony Musso, Don Kording, Bill Foster, Nick Passomato, John Mule.

Catchers

George Fuiten

Mike Fenton

78

Left to right: Chris Farrell, Dennis Swick, Jim Nail, Terry Etling, Mike Fenton, Dave Musso.

Left to right: Terry Florek, Howard Thomas, Dennis Korte, Jerry Boner.

OUTFIELDERS

Maureen Rawley
Captain

Peggy Garrett

Vara Best

Jackie Svanda

Melissa Loy

Sally Verton

Janis Silverman

ll Forbes, John Streb. ROW TWO: Nick
ROW THREE: Jack Farrow, Brian Finn,

Ferox: ROW ONE: (left to right) Brad Hoyt, Mike Howie, Dave Rose, Mike Fenton, Grey
Geminn, Glen Sudol. ROW TWO: Jerry Boner, George Fuiten, Greg Snyder, Steve Romack,
Nick Tropiano, Lee Wright, Perry Martz. ROW THREE: Jerry Zimmerman, Steve Carlson,
Chris Farrell, Marty Dial, Ken Alepra, Bob Bridges, Bruce Hogan, Mike Przybyl.

Ferox Captures I.M. Basketball Championship

KNEELING: (left to right) Bruce Hogan, Nick Tropiano, Steve Carlson, Dave Hamplemon, Mike Fenton, Mike Howie.
STANDING: Jay Hodges, Greg Snyder, Chris Farrell, Grey Gemmin, Mike Przybyl, George Fuiten, Dave Rose, Brad Hoyt.

**Ferox-Walton
Co-Champs
I.M. Soccer**

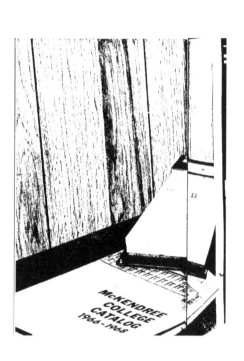

McKENDREE
COLLEGE
CATALOG
1966 - 1968

Student Congress

1st ROW: Left to Right; Wieland Roeschman, David Rose, Rick Newbury, Bill Lirely, Jerry Boner, Martha Scully, Craig Moore, John Fenoli, Larry A. Schmalenberger. 2nd ROW: Anna McNeely, Linda Walton, Billye Parker, Vara Best, John McCormack, Mike Howie, Gary Gehrs, Valeria Burton, Judy Herrin, Robert Drews, Wesley Berg, Lauren Fowler, Allison Taylor. 3rd ROW: Gary Dollinger, Bruce Hogan, Brad Hoyt, Fred Hawker, Tom Sanders, Nick Passomato, Karen Nottrott.

Executive Council

1st ROW: Left to Right; Linda Walton, Robert Drews, Valeria Burton. 2nd ROW: John Fenoli, Mary Cox, Dave Cornelius, Judy Herrin, Jerry Zimmerman.

Student Welfare

Academic Council

1st ROW: Left to Right; Karen Nottrott, John McCormack. 2nd ROW: Rick Newbury, Tom Sanders, Wes Berg.

Student Congress is the body charged with the responsibility of being, not only the voice of the students, but the liaison between the Student Body and faculty and administration. As prescribed by his Constitution, the President of Student Congress is to act as spokesman for the Congress and the Student Body to the Faculty and Administration.

Campus Program Board

Executive Committee

Top to Bottom: Vicki Coleman, Diane George, Margo Rutledge, Rose Harris, David Wilkey, Lauren Fowler, Sheri Smith, Ralph Miller, Cletus Davis.

Speaker's Committee

1st ROW: Left to Right; Criag Moore, Margaret Lorentzen, Phil Marcell. 2nd ROW: Chip Murray, Ruth Anderson, John McCormack.

Films Committee

Names start bottom center and go toward the left: Wesley Decker, Jane Templeton, Brain Finn, Melissa Loy, Ken Westlund, Steve McFall, Diane George.

Publicity Committee

Left to Right: John McCormack, Ruth Anderson, Rick Carpenter, Rose Harris, David Wilkey.

SEATED Left to Right: Debbie Upchurch, Peggy Garrett, Margaret Lorentzen. STANDING: Cindy Upchurch, Rose Harris, Margo Rutledge, Susan Towers.

Hospitality Committee

Recreation Committee

FRONT: Left to Right; Byron Calvert, Lee Wright, Karen Nottrott. 2nd ROW: Beverly Terry, Tom Sanders, Ralph Miller.

Coffee House Committee

1st ROW: Left to Right; Bob Barron, Neil Caplin, Rick Carpenter. 2nd ROW: John McCormack, Don Bogue, Ruth Anderson, Cindy Upchurch, Kathy Kenyon, Hayden Davis, Lynn Grove, Richard Sternberg. 3rd ROW: Al D'Hautecourt, Paul Hirsch.

Religious Life Committee

1st ROW (Kneeling) Left to Right: Margo Rutledge, Diane George, Melissa Loy, Anna McNeely, Sally Verton, Peg Kuttin. 2nd ROW (Standing) Grey Geminn, Cindy DeHart, Jane Templeton, Linda Elvers, Cindy Upchurch. LADDER (Bottom Left to Top and Down Right): Keith Wiig, Wesley Decker, Wieland. Roeschmann, Perry Martz, David Wilkey, Jack Harkins, Al d'Hautecourt.

The Campus Program Association, a student organization, performs several functions at McKendree. The association provides films, recreation, fine arts, social life, hospitality, religious life, public relations, and speaker programs throughout the school year for the campus community to enjoy. All students have the opportunity to be put on one or more of the eight committees and have a voice in the nature of the programs and services provided by the association. All matters concerning the association are ruled on by one or more of the committees, getting a cross-section of campus opinion before any action is taken. The Association is headed by our president who is elected in an all campus election by the students. Along with the president we have eight committee chairman and a staff adviser.

The Campus Program association is a student organization using student funds for activities to benefit the students. This year at McKendree has been a most successful one for the association.

1st ROW: Left to Right; Don Bogue, Allison Taylor, Linda Meredith, Kathy Kenyon, Paul Meffert, David Durham. 2nd ROW: Linda Shawver, Sandra Ward. 3rd ROW: John Rothwell, Cletus Davis, Rick Newbury, Mark Baldwin, Richard Sternberg.

WOMEN'S JUDICIAL BOARD

Left to Right: Denise Morlan, Jane Templeton, Sandra Ward, Pat Knop, Dean Husted, Mary Cox, Karen Nottrott.

Investment Club

Left to Right: Jim Etherton, Thomas Bailey, Ralph Miller, Peggy Arnett, Vincent Drexelius, Howard Rogers, John White.

1st ROW: Left to Right (Bottom); Martha Scully, Susan Dalton, Gary Dollinger. 2nd ROW: Charlotte Ballance, Rosemarie Maloney, Denise Morlan, Elizabeth Powell. 3rd ROW: Rita Brutto, Linda Shawver, Linda Meredith, Delores Hayer. 4th ROW: Teri Kennedy, Betsy Doerwald, Ed Wegner, Vicki Wegner. 5th ROW: James Drechen, Judy Herrin, Blanche Tibbetts, Dr. Marty. 6th ROW: Phil Marcell, John Streb.

This organization was established by students preparing to be teachers. Its aims are to develop professional attitudes, to give access to professional publications, to acquaint the students with problems and techniques in teaching and provide an opportunity for socialization among those who expect to become teachers.

SEA Officers
Left to Right: Elizabeth
Powell, Susan Dalton,
Phil Marcell, Martha
Scully, Judy Herrin.

Sigma Zeta

Officers (Sigma Zeta)
Left ro Right: Dave Cornelius,
Charles Antonelli.

SITTING, Left to Right: Miss Tusov, Dave Cornelius, Carolyn Dodds. STAND-
ING: Charles Antonelli, Tom Mottershaw, Dean Siefferman, Jim Vest, Mark
Helitbrand, Keith Wiig.

Association of Black Collegiates

ABC
1st ROW: Left to Right;
Martie Gumm, Teresa
Murphy, Al Johnson, Le-
Roy Haynes. 2nd ROW:
Eric Jenkins, Derek Hill,
Gary Tydus, John Owens,
Elmer McPherson, Clif-
ton Wells.

Psychology Club

1st ROW: Left to Right; Sally Short, Margaret Lorentzen, Nancy Gohmert, Dan Williams, Kay Buehne, Elizabeth Powell, Susan Knecht. 2nd ROW: Mike Selby, Alan Fisher, Robert Clark, Mike Howie, George Taylor, Jerry Boner, Ed Wegner, Russ Smith, Anthony Musso, Charles L. Alcorn.

Psychology Club Officers:
Left to Right: Kay Buehne, Dan Williams, Nancy Gohmert.

History Club

Left to Right STANDING: Gary Moergen, Don Klienerd, Dan Friz, Blanche Laff, Rick Newbury, Rosemarie Maloney, Dave Rose, Gary Gehrs, Martha Scully, Mark Reich, Tom Mottershaw, Jim Hogeveen, Mr. Cole. KNEELING: John Kraner, Jerry Meyer.

Officers Left to Right: Rick Newbury, Rosemarie Maloney, Dave Rose, Gary Gehrs.

Women's Society of Christian Service

ROW 1: Left to Right; Linda Rezba, Linda Meredith, Sandy Ward, Linda Shawver, Susan Towers, Mrs. Gray. ROW 2: Marion Zeisset, Charlotte Ballance, Denise Morlan, Peggy Arnett, Dorothy DeVor.

Members of the Women's Society of Christian Service on the campus work with the local Methodist Church to further the Christian spirit and to help needy persons in the United States and foreign missions.

Officers: Top to Bottom: Linda Shawver, Denise Morlan, Marion Zeisset, Peggy Arnett.

Lettermen

1st ROW: Left to Right; Jim Nail, Bob Wenderoth, Mike Finley, Terry Florek, Steve McFall. 2nd ROW: Anthony Musso, Max Hook, Mike Fenton, Chris Farrel, Dean Jackson. 3rd ROW: Paul Funkhouser, Chris Farrel.

Lettermen Officers: Left to Right: Dennis Korte, Mike Finley, Paul Funkhouser, Chris Farrel.

The purpose of the Letterman's Club is to set goals which varsity letter winners may attain through club activities. The goals for which the club shall work are: (1) to establish an honor's club; (2) to recognize academic achievement of varsity athletes; (3) to promote a good image of the college through good sportsmanship and good appearance at all times; (4) to provide a means for varsity athletes to assist in the McKendree sports program and general institutional quality to the college and public; (5) to promote the good health habits inherent in an efficient sports program; (6) to emphasize the moral responsibilities of McKendree athletes by setting an example for youth on and off campus.

McKendree Choir

1st ROW: Left to Right; Dorothy Devor, Diane George, Melinda Hicks, Sandra Elliott, Peg Garrett, Margaret Lorentzen, Anna McNeely, Pat Georg: 2nd ROW: Joy Fauss, Kathy Kenyon, Barbara North, Pat North, Peg Kuttin, Teri Kennedy, Connie King, Marion Zeisset, Lauren Fowler. 3rd ROW: Michael Tribuzzi, Gary Dollinger, Larry Hauschild, Dave Schreier, Steve Hamilton, Allison Taylor, Dave Sherbondy, Fred Habermehl, David McKenzie. 4th ROW: Bruce Roper, Rick Newbury, John Rothwell, Derek Hill, Mark Heltibrand, John McCormack, William Smoltz, Ernest Lowery, Jim Kirchner.

Chapel Choir

1st ROW: Left to Right; Dave Sherbondy, Allison Taylor, Peg Garrett, Joy Fauss. 2nd ROW: Cletus Davis, Ernest Lowery, Sandra Elliott, Dorothy Devor. 3rd ROW: Rick Newbury, Derek Hill, Gary Dollinger, Anna McNeely, Connie King. 4th ROW: Lauren Fowler, Pat Georg.

Officers:
1st ROW: Left to Right; Cletus Davis, Pat North. 2nd ROW: Sandra Elliott, Kathy Kenyon, Connie King, Pat Georg.

McKendree Review

Left to Right SITTING: Joe Kyle, Greg Snyder, Dave Rose. STANDING: Rich Aubuchon, Jerry Zimmerman, Margo Rutledge, Sharman Hehn, Jim Etherton, Rick Newbury.

Left to Right: Joe Kyle, Greg Snyder, Dave Rose.

Speech

Reader's Theater

Left to Right: Will Roeschmann, Pat North, John McCormack, Rick Carpenter, Bill Smoltz, Craig Moore, Kathi Meggs, Barbara North, Joy Fauss, Mr. Thomlison.

Kathi Meggs, Treasurer; Craig Moore, Secretary; Bill Smoltz, Vice President; John McCormack, President.

Pi Kappa Delta

STANDING, Left to Right: Mr. Thomlison, Rick Carpenter, Bill Smoltz, Dave Gross. SEATED: Kathi Meggs, Pat North.

Pat North, Vice President; Bill Smoltz, President; Kathi Meggs, Secretary-Treasurer.

FIRST ROW: Mr. Thomlison, David Gross, Helen Stroup, Barbara North, Mel Roberts, Will Roeschmann. SECOND ROW: Craig Moore, John McCormack, Rick Carpenter, Kathi Meggs.

OND ROW: Rick Carpenter, President; Craig Moore, Treasurer.

Alpha Psi Omega

FIRST ROW: Kathi Meggs, Lauren Fowler, Mrs. Welch. SECOND ROW: Will Roeschmann, Rick Carpenter, Jim Etherton, John McCormack, Bill Smoltz, Mr. Thomlison.

Kathi Meggs, Vice President; Lauren Fowler, President; John McCormack, Secretary-Treasurer.

McKendrean Staff

TOP TO BOTTOM:
Clete Davis, Robert
Bridges, Dave Cor-
nellus, Mr. Carl
Stockton, Rich Au-
buchon, Cindy De-
Hart, Jane Temple-
ton, Linda Goetz,
Mary Cox, Sonja
Funkhouser, Sandra
Ward, Diane George.

Photographers; Cliff Dawson and Rich Aubuchon.

Organizations Editors;
Diane George and
Cindy DeHart.

Class Editors: Sonja Funkhouser, Fresh.; Sandra Ward, Soph.; Clete
Davis, Jr.; Dave Cornelius, Sr. and Who's Who.

Typists; Peggy Garrett, Kathie Watson, Margaret Lorentzen, LaVerne McCoy.

Delta Phi Sigma

FIRST ROW: Mr. Zamrazil, Gene Keck, Angelo Rizzo, John Pappageorge, Brian DeWolf, Dennis Swick. SECOND ROW: Mike Hampton, Dan Stewart, Roger Hodgson, Rick Schutta, Bob Hunter, John Stanton, Keith Wiig. THIRD ROW: Mike Johnson, John Streb, Nick Passomato, Brian Finn.

Adelphi Social-Service Society, commonly known as Delta Phi Sigma, is a relatively new organization on the McKendree campus. Founded in March of 1966 and chartered in May of 1969, Adelphi has worked to become what is now one of McKendree's leading fraternal organizations.

The 1968-69 school year has been an exciting one for the men of Adelphi. Having a widely diverse group of able young men, several have sought and achieved prominent positions on campus. This same group has contributed much to all areas of our college life through its donations of time and energy.

John Streb, Roger Hodgson, Gene Keck, Rick Schutta, Brian Finn.

Alpha Kappa Tau

KNEELING: Joseph Zalar, Fred Hawker. FIRST ROW: Harry Lilli, James Hogeveen, Dr. Sturm, Tom Mottershaw, Randy Schempp. SECOND ROW: Richard Monitto, Marc Reich, James Schulz, Ronald Copeland, Tom Roach, Carl Arkema, Bill Marlin, Terry Etling, Richard Eichkorn. THIRD ROW: Richard Nicholas, Dave Schreier, Mark Gentry, Jack Hamlin, Pat Myers, Chuck Rudiger, Tom Packard, Michael Cour.

Alpha Kappa Tau, a recently chartered organization on McKendree's campus, strives to serve the college in every aspect possible and to promote a social environment for all.

Jim Hogeveen, Vice President; Tom Mottershaw, President; Bill Marlin, Pledge Trainer; Marc Reich, Treasurer.

Kappa Lambda Iota

FIRST ROW: Terri Kennedy, Betsy Doerwald, Mary Cox, Joy Fauss, Peggy Garrett, Bernice Svada. SECOND ROW: Pat Deloney, Carol Craley, Maggie Lorentzen, Jackie Svanda, Debbie Upchurch, Barb Bowyer. THIRD ROW: Iris Houston, Gaylan Rosenberger, Maureen Rawley, Diane George, Vicki Kennedy. FOURTH ROW: Lissa Loy, Sue Sobol, Linda Elvers, Cindy Upchurch, Jane Templeton. FIFTH ROW: Anna McNeely, Sally Verton, Ruth Anderson, Virginia Brown, Ellen McWard, Margo Rutledge, Vicki Coleman. SIXTH ROW: Linda Goetz, Pat North, Peg Kuttin, Margie Tebbe, Sandra Elliott. SEVENTH ROW: Jane Misgades, Valerie Moore, Janet Brand, Pat Knop, Barb Neimier.

The Clionian Literary Society, or "Clio" as it is known, is a women's society open by invitation to any girl with a 2.00 or better cumulative grade point average.

Clio was founded in 1869 as the first society for women on McKendree's campus. As McKendree has developed and grown through the years, and Clio with it, the Clionians have strived for learning as well as college and self-betterment. Through the literary, service, and social endeavors of its members, Clio has successfully remained one of the leading societies on campus.

FIRST ROW: Pat Knop, Jackie Svanda, Diane George. SECOND ROW: Betsy Doerwald, Cindy Upchurch, Jane Templeton. THIRD ROW: Jane Misegades, Mary Cox, Peggy Garrett.

Phi Lambda Sigma

FRONT ROW: Steve McFall, John Watson, Neil Kaplan, Mike Rutledge, John Fenoli. SECOND ROW: Scott McKenzie, Al Johnson, Larry Norvell, Jim Etherton, Mark McKenna. THIRD ROW: Cletus Davis, John Owen, Steve Keene, Derek Hill.

Pi Lambda Tau

FRONT ROW: Dale Berry, John White, Dave Sherbondy, Al Fisher, Haydn Davis, George Taylor, Skip Merrit, Bill Melton. SECOND ROW: Jerry Clark, John Yoon, Dan Esders, Eui Park, Don Burke, Gary Dollinger, Tom Montgomery, Bob Smith, Perry Grieme, Dave Hassenflug, Chris Fox, Mr. Pence. THIRD ROW: Glen Coates, Ken Koste. FOURTH ROW: Roger Deterding, Tim Smith, Nick Hasakas, Gary Weintz, Jim Drechen, Ed Wegner, Les Scenna, Robert DeAngelis, Doug Grimm, Fred Rudy, Bill Donaldson, Terry Schmidt, Mark Davis.

The Platonian Literary Society which was founded in 1849 is one of the oldest societies west of the Alleghenies. Pi Lambda Tau was changed to a social society in 1962, and tries to be a progressive element in the social and academic life of McKendree.

Dave Sherbondy, Bob Smith, Jerry Clark, Gary Dollinger.

Phi Rho Chi

FIRST ROW "Left to Right"; Bruce Hoggan, Steve Carlson, Dave Rose, Greg Snyder, Marty Dail, Brad Hoyt, George Fuiten. SECOND ROW: Perry Martz, Jerry Zimmerman, Glen Sudol, Steve Romack, Nick Tropiano, Mike Howie, Mike Fenton, Craig Alexy, Lee Wright. THIRD ROW: Robert Bridges, Jay Hodges, Mike Prysbyl, Grey Geminn, Jerry Boner, Chris Farrel.

"Left to Right"; Greg Snyder, president; Dave Rose, vice president; Marty Dial, secretary; Steve Carlson, Treasurer.

Ferox was organized on the McKendree Campus in 1963 with the spirit of the organization emphasizing unity in strength.

The members have, through cooperative efforts, provided many activities which benefit the campus and fulfill their purpose in promoting social, athletic, and service activities.

Sigma Kappa Tau

FIRST ROW: Karen Nottrott, Kay Buehne, Barbara North, Peggy Arnett. SECOND ROW: (bottom to top) Delores Hayer, Susan Towers, Marianna Davis, Nancy Svanda, Pat Calloway, Melva Kloth, Linda Resba. THIRD ROW: Marian Zeissett, Denise Morlan, Barb Broeckling, Beverly Terry.

The Sigma Kappa Tau Society was organized as a new dimension on the McKendree campus in January of 1967. Its purpose is to promote sisterhood, service to the college and community, and scholastic achievement of its members. Through these goals the Society strives for a better relationship between the college and the community.

Karen Nottrott, Vice President; Marianna Davis, President; Bev Terry, Secretary-Treasurer.

Inter Society Council

FIRST ROW: Dean Schmalenberger, Mr. Garcia, Mrs. Snead, Mrs. Husted, Mrs. Smith, Mr. Pence, Dr. Sturm. SECOND ROW: Tom Mottershaw, Dan Strobo, Larry Norvell, Betsy Doerwald, Pat Knop, Marianna Davis, Liz Powell, Keith Wiig, Dave Rose, Greg Snyder, Bob DeAngelis, Dave Sherbondy.

The Inter Society Council, with representatives from each campus society, coordinates and assists the societies in their activities. This year the ISC successfully sponsored a Battle of the Bands and a Greek week and through many other efforts has effectively achieved a respected position on campus.

Dave Rose, Pat Knop, Dean Schmalenberger, Greg Snyder, Dan Strobo.

PRESIDENT
ERIC
RACKHAM

ERIC RACKHAM, M.A., Ph.D.
President

J. STUART MILIRON, M.S., Ed.D.
Vice President, Development

EMERIAL OWEN, Ed.M., Ph.D.
Academic Dean

121

LARRY SCHMALENBERGER, M.S.
Dean of Students

GRACE HUSTED, M.A.
Dean of Women

DAVID DURHAM, Th.M.
Chaplain

VERNON SNEAD, M.S. (Ed.)
Business Manager

FRED ROBINSON, B.A.
Assistant Business Manager

JAMES MANEKE, B.A.
Admissions Officer

VICTOR KAPETONOVIC, B.A.
Admissions Officer

LYNN GROVE, B.A., M.A.
Head Librarian

IONE PENCE, B.A.
Registrar

SHERRI SMITH, B.A.
Director of Campus Center

KENNETH JAEGER, B.S.
Director of Public Information

PHYLLIS KUHL
Adult Staff, Campus Center

BOBBIE BRYANT, R.N.
School Nurse

RUTHELLEN PEGG
Director
Communications Center

JOE BONER
Superintendent of
Buildings and Grounds

MAINTENANCE:
E. Schill, J. Fischer, T. Dawson,
B. Harmon, C. Kline, B. Stewart

DONELDA JACOLICK, M.S.
Director of Food Services

SNACK BAR STAFF:
T. Vorus, O. Haeuber, M. Mandely.

MARCELLA KECK
Bookstore Manager

COOKS:
G. Nailing I. Trame,
R. Brown, D. Nunn,
F. Burns, M. Webster,
E. Boone, M. Iberg.

LIBRARY CLERKS:
Margaret Packard, Mary Berguist, Evelyn Cummins.

OFFICE PERSONNEL:
Erma Murphy, Doris Weber, Gail Reno, Virginia Pepper, Lena Graham, Audrey Schiefer.

SECRETARIES:
FRONT ROW: Cheryl MacMinn, Alma Weik, Nancy Snead. MIDDLE ROW: Chris Becker, Doris Wolfslau, Bonnie Robinson. BACK ROW: Mary Booth, Betty White, Lorraine Brownfield.

Men's Residence Staff

FRONT ROW: Bob Stankus, HR Walton; Bob Wenderoth, HR Walton; Ralph Miller, RA Walton; Dave Cornelius, RA Walton. BACK ROW: Tom Sanders, HR Baker; Dave Bailey, HR Carnegie; Mike Howie, RA Baker; Bruce Hogan, RA Carnegie; Steve Carlson, RA Baker.

Women's Residence Staff

Karen Nottrott, HR Clark; Lauren Fowler, RA Clark; Cindy Upchurch, RA Barnett; Liz Powell, RA Barnett; Dee Hayer, RA Barnett.

The Division of

SOCIAL STUDIES

ROLAND RICE, S.T.B., Ph.D.
Division Chairman
Professor, Philosophy of Religion

OTHA CLARK, B.D., Ph.D.
Professor, History

DWAYNE COLE, M.A.
Assistant Professor, History

ES

ROBERT BROWN, M.A.
Assistant Professor, Sociology

CARL STOCKTON, B.S., S.T.B.
Instructor, History

RALPH SCHARNAU, M.A.
Assistant Professor, History

CARROL LEAS, M.B.A.
Assistant Professor,
Business Administration

HOWARD L. ROGERS, M.A.
Assistant Professor,
Economics and Political Science

ELDON DITTEMORE, M.S.
Assistant Professor,
Economics and Business

Division of

LANGUAGES AND LITERATURE

EUGENE SEUBERT, M.A.
Instructor, English

DAVID PACKARD, M.S.
Division Chairman
Assistant Professor, English

GRACE WELCH, M.S.
Instructor, English

MARGURITE SKAAR, M.A.
Instructor, French

TERRY THOMLISON, M.A.
Instructor, Speech

HAROLD HUCH, M.S. (Ed.)
Lecturer, Spanish

MARINO GARCIA, M.A.
Instructor, Spanish

FRANCE DIXON
Tutor, French and German

137

The Division of

FINE ARTS

GLENN FREINER, M.M.
Division Chairman
Associate Professor, Music

WILLIAM HODGE, M.F.A.
Associate Professor, Art

ORVILLE SCHANZ, M.M.
Assistant Professor, Music and Art

GEORGE TUERCK
Lecturer

STEPHANIE OWEN, M.M.
Assistant Professor, Music and Piano

Division of

SCIENCE AND
MATHEMATICS

FRED FLEMING, M.S.
Division Chairman
Professor, Biology

MYRON REESE, Ph.D.
Assistant Professor, Chemistry

ROBERT VAN DAN ELZEN, M.S.
Instructor, Mathematics

JOANNE TUSOV, M.S.
Instructor,
Chemistry and Biology

VICTOR GUMMERSHEIMER, M.S.
Instructor, Mathematics

TOBY WARD, M.A.
Instructor, Physics

**DIRECTOR OF
SPECIAL STUDENTS**

ROY STURM, St.B., M.A., Ph.D.
Professor

The Division of

TEACHER PREPARATION

RALPH MARTY, M.S., Ed.D.
Division Chairman
Professor, Education

CURTIS L. TRAINER, M.S., Ed.D.
Associate Professor, Education

BLANCHE TIBBETTS, M.S.
Assistant Professor, Education

CHARLES ALCORN, M.A.
Associate Professor,
Psychology

HARRY M. STATHAM, M.S.
Coach, Physical Education

KATHERINE KIRTS, M.A.
Instructor, Physical Education

FIRST ROW: Paul Sims, Rayburn Fox, Eric Rackham, Milburn Akers, Charles Daily, W. P. Mautz, Harold Hanser, George Hand, Jack Travelstead. SECOND ROW: Robert Krause, Billy Hahs, Mrs. Ralph Hill, David Hardy, Robert White, Mrs. Homer Luttrell, Ernest Britton, Donald Lowe. THIRD ROW: Adolph Unruh, Robert Woodward, Donald Wilson, Ernest Karandjeff, Max Goldenberg, Walt Ackermann, Charles Richards, Joseph Lowery, Ed Bott, Ira Thetford.

EXECUTIVE COUNCIL

Paul Sims, Charles Daily, Milburn Akers (Chm.), W. P. Mautz, Eric Rackham, George Hand, Jack Travelstead, Rayburn Fox.

Milburn Akers, Eric Rackham.

Charles Antonelli
Christopher, Illinois
Major: Biology
Minor: Philosophy

Peggy Arnett
Texico, Illinois
Major: Business
Minor: Economics

Vicki Coleman
Percy, Illinois
Clio
Student Conduct Committee
President's Advisory Committee
Campus Program Board President
Cheerleader
Inter-Society Council

Judy Beasley
Caseyville, Illinois
Major: Elementary Education
Minor: Psychology

Robert Bridges
Chicago, Illinois
Major: Sociology
Minor: Physical Education

Sandra Brock

Neil Caplin
N. Valley Stream, L.I., New York
Major: Fine Arts
Minor: Education

Vicki Lynn Coleman
Percy, Illinois
Major: Elementary Education
Minor: Physical Education

Patti Knop
Clio President
1968 Homecoming Queen Candidate
Inter-Society Council
Films Committee
Women's Judicial Board

David Wayne Cornelius
Cleveland, Ohio
Major: Biology
Minor: Chemistry--Psychology

Steven Crews
Fairfield, Illinois
Major: Business
Minor: History

David Homer Wilkey
Student Congress
McKendree Crown Investment League
Phi Beta Lambda Business Fraternity
Calendar Committee
Campus Program Board
Homecoming Parade Chairman 1968

Carolyn Dodds
St. Louis, Missouri
Major: Mathematics
Minor: Sociology

Betsy Doerwald
Newton, New Jersey
Major: Elementary Education
Minor: Sociology

Gary Dollinger
Troy, Illinois
Major: Piano
Minor: Voice--Education

Vincent Drexelius
Edwardsville, Illinois
Major: Business
Minor: Psychology

Daniel Truman Esders
Olney, Illinois
Major: Elementary Education
Minor: History

Alan Fisher
Springfield, Illinois
Major: Psychology
Minor: Biology

Terry Lee Florek
East St. Louis, Illinois
Major: Business
Minor: Economics

George Fuiten
Virden, Illinois
Major: English
Minor: Physical Education

Charles Fulkerson
Belleville, Illinois
Major: Social Studies
Minor: Sociology

David Killam
Adelphi Vice-President and Treasurer
Student Congress
Varsity Baseball
Intermurals

Gary Lee Gehrs
Carlyle, Illinois
Major: History
Minor: Sociology

Grey Geminn
Belleville, Illinois
Major: Business
Minor: Sociology

Elizabeth Doerwald
Clio
Dean's List
1968 Homecoming Queen Candidate
Barnett Hall (Vice-President)
Inter-Society Council
Student Education Association
Cheerleader
Women's Intermurals

Gerald Gaa
Belleville, Illinois
Major: Business
Minor: Economics

Ronald Gregory
Sauget, Illinois
Major: Chemistry
Minor: Psychology

Fred Robert Habermehl
Dupo, Illinois
Major: Business
Minor: Sociology

Barbara North
Stage Crafters
Alphi Psi Omega
Debate Club
Grandy Scholar
Charter President, Sigma Kappa Tau
Student Congress
Spanish Club

Jay Edward Hodges
Girard, Illinois
Major: Social Studies Divisional
Minor: History Core

Richard Houghland
Pinckneyville, Illinois
Major: Chemistry
Minor: Mathematics

John Fenoli
Philo Corresponding Secretary
Student Congress Welfare Committee Chairman
Campus Program Board Planning Committee
Ad Hoc Faculty-Student Chapel Committee
Student Congress Church-School Relationship Committee

Wendell Johnson
Lebanon, Illinois
Major: Physical Education
Minor: Business

Herbert Alan Kaiserman
Springfield, Illinois
Major: Physical Education
Minor: Psychology

Teri Kennedy
Cahokia, Illinois
Major: Elementary Education
Minor: Sociology

David Wendell Kitlam
Hartford, Illinois
Major: Mathematics
Minor: Business

Susan VanDanElzen Knecht
Collinsville, Illinois
Major: Psychology
Minor: Biology

Patricia Knop
Campbell Hill, Illinois
Major: Elementary Education
Minor: Physical Education

Joseph Kyle
Decatur, Illinois
Major: Social Studies Divisional
Minor: History Core

Frances Layfield
Troy, Illinois
Major: Elementary Education
Minor: English

Rosemarie Maloney
Dahlgren, Illinois
Major: History
Minor: Mathematics

Sandra Kay Hampton
Student Congress
Dean's List
Homecoming Attendant
Clio, Past Secretary

Steve McFall
Collinsville, Illinois
Major: Physical Education
Minor: Speech

Mary Ann Miller
Centralia, Illinois
Major: Sociology
Minor: Psychology

Kathi Meggs
Freeburg, Illinois
Major: Speech
Minor: Business

Ralph Miller
Normal, Illinois
Major: Business,
Minor: Economics

Gary Moergen
Belleville, Illinois
Major: Social Studies Divisional
Minor: History Core

Denise Elizabeth Morlan
Mt. Vernon, Illinois
Major: Social Studies Divisional
Minor: History Core

George Morris
Belleville, Illinois
Major: Biology
Minor: History

James Nail
O'Fallon, Illinois
Major: Physical Education
Minor: Biology

Mohamad Nazem
Nishabour, Meshed, Iran
Major: Chemistry
Minor: Mathematics

George Fuiten
Ferox Past President and Vice-President
Inter-Society Council Chairman
Lettermen's Club Vice-President
Baseball
Intramurals
Student Conduct Committee
Sigma Tau Delta
Ad Hoc Committee on Student Rights
Dean's List
Best Dressed Man on Campus

Barbara Niemeier
Tallula, Illinois
Major: Elementary Education
Minor: Psychology

Gerald Nixon
Divernon, Illinois
Major: Business
Minor: Psychology

Barbara Ellen North
Lebanon, Illinois
Major: Speech
Minor: Psychology

Karen Nottrott
Dupo, Illinois
Major: Physical Education
Minor: Psychology

Glenn Roland Oliphant
West Caldwell, New Jersey
Major: Business
Minor: Economics

Gary Gehrs
History Club
Historian Reporter
Student Congress
Faculty Committee on Student Life

George Hugh Poston
Wood River, Illinois
Major: Science Divisional
Minor: Chemistry Core

Elizabeth Ann Powell
Springfield, Illinois
Major: Elementary Education
Minor: Psychology

Stephen Romack
Decatur, Illinois
Major: Mathematics
Minor: Economics

David Joseph Rose
Canton, Ohio
Major: History
Minor: Sociology

Roger Warren Russell
Granite City, Illinois
Major: Social Studies Divisional
Minor: Sociology Core

Thomas Sanders
Toledo, Illinois
Major: Social Studies Divisional
Minor: Sociology Core

Martha Inez Scully
Springfield, Ohio
Major: Speech
Minor: History

Barbara Smith
Danville, Illinois
Major: Social Studies Divisional
Minor: Sociology Core

Robert Smith
St. Louis, Missouri
Major: Business
Minor: Speech

William James Smoltz
Colorado Spring, Colorado
Major: Speech
Minor: Art

Russell Duane Smith
Ashland, Illinois
Major: Philosophy
Minor: Psychology

Gregory Snyder
Calumet City, Illinois
Major: Business
Minor: Economics

Robert Peter Stankus
St. Louis, Missouri
Major: Business
Minor: Economics

Susan Towers
Belleville, Illinois
Major: Elementary Education
Minor: Art

Joyce Tracy
Granite City, Illinois
Major: Elementary Education
Minor: Psychology

Nicholas Tropiano
Philadelphia, Pennsylvania
Major: Business
Minor: Psychology

Roberta O'Hear Trotter
Charleston, South Carolina
Major: Art
Minor: Psychology

James Vest
O'Fallon, Illinois
Major: Chemistry
Minor: Biology

Marianna Davis Tucci
New Baden, Illinois
Major: Physical Education
Minor: History

Edward William Wegner
Lombard, Illinois
Major: Psychology
Minor: Biology

Keith Wilg
Lincolnwood, Illinois
Major: Mathematics
Minor: Business

David Homer Wilkey
Nashville, Illinois
Major: Business
Minor: Economics

Dan Williams
Venice, Illinois
Major: Philosophy
Minor: Psychology

Jerry Zimmerman
Schenectady, New York
Major: Sociology
Minor: Economics

Marion Zeisset
Edwardsville, Illinois
Major: Elementary Education
Minor: Music

Class of 1970

Judy Herron, Secretary
John Stroh, President

Phil Schwab, Treasurer
Jack Farrow, Vice-president

Mary Lou Anders
Mascoutah, Ill.

Richard Aubuchon
East St. Louis, Ill.

Wesley Berg
Chicago, Ill.

David Bergin
Decatur, Ill.

Robert Bower
Illiopolis, Ill.

Virginia Brown
St. Jacob, Ill.

Steven Buescher
Okawville, Ill.

Byron Calvert
Martinsville, Ill.

John Craner
Elkhart, Ill.

Cletus Davis
Okawville, Ill.

| Mark Davis Robinson, Ill. | Wesley Decker Pasadena, Cal. | Martin Dial Decatur, Ill. | Robert Drews New Castle, Del. | Brian Finn Peoria, Ill. |

| William Forbes Alexander, Ill. | Lauren Fowler St. Louis, Mo. | Paul Funkhouser Mt. Vernon, Ill. | Sonja Funkhouser Belleville, Ill. | Lawrence Genge Chicago, Ill. |

| Linda Gohmert Lebanon, Ill. | David Gross St. Jacob, Ill. | James Hagemann Lebanon, Ill. | Thomas Halloran Wood River, Ill. | Stephen Hamilton Lebanon, Ill. |

| Paul Havenar Lisle, Ill. | Delores Hayer Sparta, Ill. | Judith Herrin Herrin, Ill. | Kenneth Holtgreve Belleville, Ill. | Max Hook Vienna, Ill. |

Larry Hopkins
Patoka, Ill.

Lester Jackson
Lebanon, Ill.

Stephen Keene
Lewistown, Ill.

Dennis Korte
Lebanon, Ill.

Lee Ladinsky
Creve Coeur, Mo.

William Lirely
Marion, Ill.

Duane Livingston
Decatur, Ill.

Stephen McClure
Flat Rock, Ill.

John McCormack
St. Louis, Mo.

Robert McKinley
Bridgeport, Ill.

Peggy Melton
Belleville, Ill.

Jerry Meyer
Coulterville, Ill.

Larry Mooney
Dix, Ill.

Anthony Musso
Belleville, Ill.

Perry Newbury
DuQuoin, Ill.

Thomas Packard
Staunton, Ill.

Steven Pearson
Mt. Vernon, Ill.

Cecil Penn
Dow, Ill.

Maureen Rawley
East St. Louis, Ill.

Linda Rezba
Sparta, Ill.

Dereatha Rhoades
Sullivan, Ill.

James Richardson
Pontiac, Ill.

Wieland Roeschmann
Middleville, N.J.

Michael Rutledge
Arthur, Ill.

Peter Saineghi
Christopher, Ill.

Floyd Schutta
Orchard Park, N.Y.

Philip Schwab
Litchfield, Ill.

Linda Shawver
Lewistown, Ill.

David Sherbondy
Cleveland Heights, O.

Robert Shook
Mascoutah, Ill.

Robert Siefferman
Troy, Ill.

Rick Stahl
Smithton, Ill.

Audrey Steinkamp
Okawville, Ill.

David Stepp
East Carondelet, Ill.

John Streb
Dobbs Ferry, N.Y.

Helen Stroup
Carbondale, Ill.

Jacqueline Svanda
Steeleville, Ill.

Nancy Svanda
Sparta, Ill.

George Taylor
Alton, Ill.

Marjorie Tebbe
Highland, Ill.

Jane Templeton
Pinckneyville, Ill.

Beverly Terry
Venice, Ill.

William Truty
Ottawa, Ill.

Vicki Wegner
Lebanon, Ill.

Robert Wenderoth
Milford, Ohio

John White
Decatur, Ill.

David Williams
Mt. Olive, Ill.

Lee Wright
Girard, Ill.

172

Class of 1971

...wie, Student Congress Rep.; Al Johnson, President; Barbara Bower, Secretary.

| Thomas Bailey | Mark Baldwin | George Baver | Robert Bennett | R. Dale Berry |
| Knoxville, Ill. | Pana, Ill. | Pennsburg, Pa. | Birmingham, Mich. | Albion, Ill. |

| Vara L. Best | Barbara Bowyer | Stephen Carlson | Don Clinard | Carol Craley |
| Livingston, Ill. | West Frankfort, Ill. | Galesburg, Ill. | Butler, Ill. | Brookhaven, Pa. |

Cynthia DeHart
Taylorville, Ill.

Patricia Deloney
St. Louis, Mo.

Alain D'Hautecourt
Yonkers, N.Y.

Deborah Dodds
Clayton, Mo.

Linda Elvers
Gillespie, Ill.

Donna Emerick
Wood River, Ill.

Terry Etling
Mascoutah, Ill.

Joy Fauss
Belleville, Ill.

S. Michael Fenton
Gillespie, Ill.

Peggy Garrett
St. Louis, Mo.

S. Diane George
Carbondale, Ill.

Sally Gillespey
Collinsville, Ill.

Linda Goetz
Fairview Park, O.

Robert Greene
Mt. Vernon. Ill.

David Hassenflug
St. Georges, Bermuda

LeRoy Haynes
Bronx, N.Y.

174

Paul Hirsch
Mineola, N.Y.

Roger Hodgson
Freeport, N.Y.

R. Bruce Hogan
Pleasant Plains, Ill.

Michael Howie
Chester, Ill.

Bradley Hoyt
Mt. Prospect, Ill.

Laura Jensen
Granite City, Ill.

Kathleen Kenyon
El Paso, Ill.

James Kirchner
Springfield, Ill.

Blanche Laff
Yonkers, N.Y.

Leslie Lieberstein
Palos Park, Ill.

Kimberly Littell
Park Ridge, Ill.

Margaret Lorentzen
Red Bud, Ill.

Ernest Lowery
DuQuoin, Ill.

Melissa Loy
Kinmundy, Ill.

Gloria Mannz
Troy, Ill.

Warren McCollom
White Hall, Ill.

Scott McKenzie
Decatur, Ill.

Ellen McWard
Taylorville, Ill.

Paul Meffert
Highland, Ill.

Julia Misegades
East St. Louis, Ill.

Thomas Montgomery
Rosemont, Pa.

Valerie Moore
St. Louis, Mo.

David Mueller
Chester, Ill.

Karen Mueller
Wilmette, Ill.

George Myers
Wolf Lake, Ill.

Lester Nalevac
Bellwood, Ill.

Deborah Nevois
Collinsville, Ill.

Margaret Osterhage
Waterloo, Ill.

Billye Parker
Fairfield, Ill.

Michaeline Ricchiardi
Gillespie, Ill.

Gaylan Rosenberger
Jacksonville, Ill.

John Rothwell
Galveston, Ind.

James Schulz
New Athens, Ill.

Sally Short
Salem, Ill.

176

| Suzanne Sobol
Lebanon, Ill. | Dan Stewart
Robinson, Ill. | Bernice Svanda
Steeleville, Ill. | Mary Beth Tompkins
Leroy, Ill. | Cynthia Upchurch
Dupo, Ill. |

| Debbie Upchurch
Cahokia, Ill. | Sally Verton
Gillespie, Ill. | Sandra Ward
Newton, Ill. | John Watson
Pensacola, Fla. | Kenneth Westlund
Rockford, Ill. |

Paul Widicus
St. Jacob, Ill.

Joseph Zalar
Litchfield, Ill.

Class of 1972

Phil Ambers
Collinsville, Ill.

Ruth Anderson
St. Louis, Mo.

Robert Barron
Cinnaminson, N.J.

Edward Belva
McLeansboro, Ill.

Kathleen Berg
Newport, N.Y.

Janet Brand
Piscataway, N.J.

Margaret Branson
Mattoon, Ill.

Donald Burke
Kankakee, Ill.

Valeria Burton
Philadelphia, Pa.

| Jack Clark | Paula Covey | Smith Cruit | Hayden Davis | Linda Everett |
| Columbia, Ill. | Springfield, Ill. | Dalton City, Ill. | Springfield, Ill. | Jacksonville, Ill. |

| Ruth Finney | Chris Fox | Rita Fryman | James German | Perry Grieme |
| Virden, Ill. | Godfrey, Ill. | Mattoon, Ill. | Cottage Hills, Ill. | Elkhart, Ill. |

| John Harkins | Richard Hartnett | Larry Hauschild | Milinda Hicks | Derek Hill |
| Brooklyn, N.Y. | Lackawanna, N.Y. | Gillespie, Ill. | Pinckneyville, Ill. | Cairo, Ill. |

| John Hinman | Loren Hoffman | Iris Houston | Connie King | Melva Kloth |
| Mound City, Ill. | Sparta, Ill. | Cleveland, O. | Lebanon, Ill. | Sparta, Ill. |

Peggy Kuttin
New Douglas, Ill.

Steven Laur
Bridgeport, Ill.

Alice Lingafelter
Hutsonville, Ill.

Wayne Loehring
Summerfield, Ill.

Rhonda Lurtz
O'Fallon, Ill.

Mark McKenna
Mystic, Conn.

G. David McKenzie
Vienna, Ill.

Anna McNeely
Tower Hill, Ill.

Bill Melton
West York, Ill.

Joyce Miller
Anna, Ill.

David Moe
Dacca, Pakistan

Phil Morgan
Metropolis, Ill.

Thomas Mueller
Highwood, Ill.

John Mule
Trenton, N.J.

Theresa Murphy
Chicago, Ill.

David Musso
Belleville, Ill.

Pat North
Lebanon, Ill.

Gary Norvich
Madison, Ill.

Jerrold Olmstead
Toledo, Ill.

Juvata Orr
Jonesboro, Ill.

Suzanne Phillips
Collinsville, Ill.

Gary Plum
St. Elmo, Ill.

Michael Przybyl
Syracuse, N.Y.

Bruce Roper
Girard, Ill.

James Sanders
Toledo, Ill.

Les Scenna
Bridgeville, Pa.

Cheryl Shaw
Bondville, Ill.

Martha Skinner
Ina, Ill.

Tim Smith
St. Louis, Mo.

Gary Stanko
Staunton, Ill.

Robert Steinman
Decatur, Ill.

Glen Sudol
Paasaic, N.J.

Allison Taylor
Marion, Ill.

Michael Tribuzzi
Buffao, N.Y.

Junichi Tsuji
Akita City, Japan

Linda Walton
Vandalia, Ill.

Gary Weintz
Christopher, Ill.

Clifton Wells
East St. Louis, Ill.

Sharon Yannotti
Lebanon, Ill.

Dedication

Kenneth Charles Frazer, son of Mr. & Mrs. Hubert Frazer, was born September 16, 1945 in Chester, Illinois. In his elementary and secondary years of schooling, Ken participated in cross country, Little League and as a class officer. Within his community, Ken was active in Church league and Boy Scouts where he achieved one of scouting's most admirable awards, that of Eagle Scout.

Upon coming to McKendree, Ken, known to many as "The Praz", made of himself a student, a diplomat, a brother, a participant in many organizations and most of all a man; a man who shall remain in the hearts of those who knew and loved him.

Ken was a sociology major and a psychology minor. He served as President and Treasurer of Phi Rho Chi, was a member of the Student Conduct Committee for two years, and was President of his sophomore class. As an athlete, Ken was a master at the game of tennis which he loved to play. He was also a member of The Letterman's Club. In service to his school, Ken represented McKendree College at two model United Nations Assemblies.

Mr. Robert Brown, Professor of Sociology, spoke of Ken as a man of "fairness and integrity whose zest and enthusiasm were an inspiration to us all". Ken gave his life for God and Country in Viet Nam, Sept. 19, 1968.

It is with this thought in mind that we, the staff of the 1969 McKendrean, dedicate this book of memories to Kenneth Charles Frazer whose memory will dwell within the hearts of many forever.

Kenneth C. Frazer

The 1968-69 school year went by fast, but many things happened and many things will be remembered. New friends were made, old acquaintances renewed and all of us added another year to our lives within a community which will come to be an important part of our growing up.

It is hoped that many will have found a turning point in their lives while at McKendree this year in many or maybe just one aspect of his or her life. If this be the case then let us be grateful for we are all very fortunate to be part of such a wonderful country that provides us with the opportunities such as we have.

One day soon everyone will reach the year of commencement and will be ready to go out and use what he has worked so hard to obtain while in college.

Going out into the world and using all the knowledge acquired in school will be of no use at all if one cannot enjoy his society and its people. Living together and enjoying life will be the blessing of anyone's life that will warm his heart and fulfill his emptiness when he senses defeat or struggle.

In closing the year, I would like to personally thank every member of my staff for the excellent job which they did, for their fine cooperation and patience through two semesters. You were all extremely helpful and I enjoyed working with each and everyone of you.

To all of the graduating seniors, I want to wish the best of luck for your success in the years to come. May you always hold fond memories of your years at McKendree.

Robert Bridges
Editor

"Success depends upon backbone, not wishbone".